C000150047

THE LONG AND THE SHORT OF IT
SENIOR MOMENTS!

If your internal monologue largely consists of three phrases:
'WHERE THE HELL IS IT?',
'SOMEBODY MUST HAVE MOVED IT'
and **'WELL, I DON'T REMEMBER LEAVING IT THERE',**
then this is the book for you.

Fix a smile, count your blessings
and live today to the fullest because tomorrow

MIGHT BE EVEN WORSE ...

• A SENIOR MOMENT IS WHEN •

Asking The Waiter To Cut Your Pizza Into Four Slices Because You Can't Possibly Eat Eight.

DON'T *PANIC!*

You're just having another SENIOR MOMENT,
but you'll have forgotten all about it in ... um ...

A **SENIOR MOMENT** IS LIKE WAITING FOR A BUS AND THEN MISSING **ALL THREE** OF THEM.

TO ERR IS HUMAN.

(To forget that your **trousers** are on your **head** is senior.)

Burn the candle at both ends? At my age?
I can't even find any matches ...

OR A CANDLE.

Offering To Babysit Your Pre-School-Age Grandchildren, Mainly For The Free Tech Support.

PREMATURE BALDNESS?

I prefer to imagine that my hair follicles
are enjoying an *early retirement*.

· A SENIOR MOMENT IS WHEN ·

YOU TRY TO FLOSS SOMEONE ELSE'S TEETH.

Every Memory Lapse Is One More Slab Of Crazy Paving On Your Path Of Rediscovery.

MEMORY IS THE RUSTY, BULLET-RIDDEN BACKPACK WE ALL DRAG AROUND WITH US.

I'VE GOT A MEMORY LIKE A ...

UM ... OH, YOU KNOW ... MESHED UTENSIL FOR STRAINING SOLIDS FROM LIQUIDS ...

A PICTURE IS WORTH A THOUSAND WORDS,
BUT A MEMORY IS ...

WAIT ... NO, IT'S GONE.

NOSTALGIA

AH, I'M SURE I USED TO REMEMBER THAT WITH A CERTAIN FONDNESS!

If memory is the gateway to happiness, my hinges are all

RUSTED UP.

• A SENIOR MOMENT IS WHEN •

JUST **THINKING** ABOUT YOUR CAR KEYS BRINGS BACK SO MANY **VIVID MEMORIES** OF PLACES WHERE THEY **AREN'T**.

IS THIS JUST A SENIOR MOMENT OR AM I LOSING MY CAMEMBERT SALOPETTES?

THE BRAIN IS AMAZING!

It starts working from the **moment** you wake up and
doesn't stop until you need to **find your glasses**.

AGE IS JUST A _NUMBER_.

In some cases, a staggeringly huge number.

YOU KNOW YOU'RE GETTING OLD WHEN YOU START TO SUSPECT THAT THE CHELSEA PENSIONERS HAVE HAD SOME WORK DONE.

I'M <u>FED</u> <u>UP</u> WITH BEING TOLD I CAN LEARN FROM MY FAILURES. I DON'T HAVE TIME. AT MY AGE I DEMAND SOME SUCCESS <u>NOW</u>!

WHEREVER THESE GOLDEN YEARS LEAD YOU, TAKE REGULAR TOILET BREAKS AND AN AMPLE SUPPLY OF MINT IMPERIALS.

AFTER A <u>NEAR-LIFETIME</u> OF SERVICE,
I THINK MY WORKING MEMORY
HAS FINALLY RETIRED AND
MOVED TO SPAIN.

Never let a senior moment diminish your pleasure
because even when you forget the words, you can still

HUM OUT OF TUNE.

As We Age, We **Grow Riper**, More Mellow And Blue-Veined – Like A Fine Stilton Or That Expensive German Cheese That **Smells Of Feet**.

• A SENIOR MOMENT IS WHEN •

YOU STAY UP <u>ALL</u> <u>NIGHT</u> WONDERING WHERE THE <u>SUN</u> WENT UNTIL, EVENTUALLY, IT <u>DAWNS</u> ON YOU.

Old age is a hell of a lot more fun than the alternative –
BEING AN ENTITLED, LETHARGIC YOUNG PERSON.

THE YEARS MAY HAVE <u>WRINKLED</u> <u>YOUR</u> <u>SKIN</u>, BUT A LONG, HOT SOAK IN THE BATH WILL GIVE YOU A <u>GLIMPSE</u> <u>OF</u> <u>HORRORS</u> YET TO COME.

I'VE GOT A MEMORY LIKE A ...

UM ... OH, YOU KNOW ... SMALL REDDISH-GOLDEN EURASIAN DEEP-BODIED FRESHWATER FISH ...

AM I WONDER WOMAN?

I **wonder** where I left my keys; I **wonder** where
I put my glasses; I **wonder** what day it is.

IF GROWING OLD CAN DAMAGE YOUR SHORT-TERM MEMORY, JUST IMAGINE THE DAMAGE GROWING OLD COULD DO.

OH, OH, WAIT! IT'S ON THE TIP OF MY TONGUE. "WHAT?", YOU MAY ASK? WELL, IF I KNEW THAT ...

· A SENIOR MOMENT IS WHEN ·

YOU LIST YOUR TOENAIL CLIPPINGS ON ETSY.

To improve my memory, my GP put me on a strict diet
that includes fatty fish, nuts and leafy greens.

IF ONLY I COULD REMEMBER WHY.

My dad suffered from

SHORT-TERM MEMORY LOSS.

I hope it doesn't run in the family because my dad suffered from

SHORT-TERM MEMORY LOSS.

THREE THINGS TO KNOW ABOUT ME:

My memory's not as **sharp** as it used to be.

Also, my memory's not as **sharp** as it used to be.

See? I've already **forgotten** the third thing.

I ATTEND A MEMORY LOSS <u>SUPPORT</u> <u>GROUP</u>. THE HOST ALWAYS BEGINS, "GOOD EVENING, YOU'RE PROBABLY ALL <u>WONDERING</u> WHY YOU'RE <u>HERE</u>."

MY SHORT-TERM MEMORY ISN'T WHAT IT USED TO BE. IT GETS ME DOWN, BUT MOST OF THE TIME I JUST TRY TO FORGET ABOUT IT.

It is during our darkest moments that we must remember where we keep the candles and the

CREAM SHERRY.

• A SENIOR MOMENT IS WHEN •

AT HOME, SITTING IMPATIENTLY ON THE BOTTOM STEP FOR AN HOUR, YOU REMEMBER THAT YOU DON'T OWN A STAIRLIFT.

EVERY WEEK, I VISIT A MEMORY SPECIALIST.

He assures me I'm making good progress, but he still insists I pay a month in advance.

IF MY MEMORY GETS ANY WORSE, I'LL BE ABLE TO THROW MYSELF A SURPRISE PARTY.

My Small, Hardy Dog Originates From <u>Tibet</u>. Sorry, I Can't Remember The Name Of Its Pure Breed, Owing To A Sudden <u>Lhasa</u> <u>Apso</u> Of <u>Memory</u>.

I don't think I got the job at the Memory Clinic.
I forgot to put a postage stamp on my application ...

OR POST IT.

I'M NOT LOSING MY SHORT-TERM MEMORY; I'M JUST GOOD AT LETTING GO OF THE RECENT PAST.

AFTER 60, THE MIND DEVELOPS A MIND OF ITS OWN.

· A SENIOR MOMENT IS WHEN ·

YOU RESOLVE TO EAT ONLY GREENS – BROCCOLI, KALE, WASABI, A PARAKEET, GARDEN HOSE, MALACHITE, ARTIFICIAL TURF, AN OLD CACTUS.

You're Only As Old As Your Eel.

No, that can't be right.
There's something *fishy* about that.

"HAVE I REMEMBERED THAT CORRECTLY?"

"What?"

"WHAT?"

"You just said, 'Have I remembered that correctly?'"

"WELL, HAVE YOU?"

MY MIND IS LIKE THE DVLA.

Information goes in, and then it's lost forever.

"MY BRAIN IS LIKE A BLACK PUDDING."
"DON'T YOU MEAN 'BLACK HOLE'?"
"WELL, IT'S USUALLY FRIED BEFORE BREAKFAST."

Fingertips, ropes, hammers, fire alarms,
campanologists, carillon players, Austrian cows ...

THEY ALL RING A BELL.

NEVER FORGET

that whatever has happened, may or may not have happened,
regardless of whether you may or may not be able to remember it.

THAT REMINDS ME ...

Where do you think my **collection of toupees** went, because, **off the top of my head**, I couldn't tell you.

MY <u>NEUROLOGIST</u> REASSURES ME THAT FOUR OUT OF FIVE SENIORS SUFFER FROM <u>MEMORY LOSS</u>. OR WAS IT <u>MEMORY</u> LOSS? I CAN'T REMEMBER. ANYWAY, IT WAS ONE OF THOSE.

I WENT JOGGING THIS MORNING.
I RAN ON THE SPOT FOR
25 MINUTES BECAUSE I FORGOT
TO OPEN THE FRONT DOOR.

One of the **benefits** of poor memory is that
every time I break wind in the bath,

I THINK IT'S A JACUZZI.

I've given up trying to improve my memory.
I'm just going to have to learn to live with it, or, rather,

WITHOUT IT.

BEFORE YOU JUDGE ME FOR HAVING A POOR MEMORY, YOU SHOULD TRY WALKING A MILE IN MY SHOES. BUT YOU'LL HAVE TO FIND THEM FIRST.

A **SENIOR MOMENT** IS LIKE WANDERING IN THE DESERT WITH AN UMBRELLA IN SEARCH OF A GIANT COCKTAIL.

YESTERDAY, I WAS DOING THE EASY CROSSWORD WHEN SUDDENLY MY MIND WENT B, BLANK, BLANK, BLANK, BLANK.

I booked a memory improvement course. It starts at 8.00 pm next Tuesday, but would you believe it? It clashes with my new

MEMORY IMPROVEMENT COURSE.

MY **COMPETITIVE BROTHER** THINKS HIS MEMORY IS BETTER THAN MINE. SO, TO WIND HIM UP, I PRETEND NOT TO **RECOGNISE HIM**. **IT'S TRUE**, BUT I'M NOT TELLING HIM THAT.

I always keep a notepad by my bed to jot down ideas.
It's empty because I can never

FIND A PEN.

DON'T REGRET THE PAST;
DON'T WORRY ABOUT THE
FUTURE; JUST TRY NOT TO DO
<u>ANYTHING</u> <u>STUPID</u> TODAY.

WHEN I'M 93,
I HOPE I'M LIVING THE DREAM.

(But not the one where I'm wearing pyjamas on the bus.)

YESTERDAY, I GOT STOPPED BY A TRAFFIC POLICE OFFICER. HIS <u>MEMORY</u> MUST BE AS <u>BAD</u> <u>AS</u> <u>MINE</u> BECAUSE HE ASKED, "DO YOU KNOW WHY I PULLED YOU OVER?"

• A SENIOR MOMENT IS WHEN •

YOU HAVE THE POWER TO CONTROL NEITHER OUTSIDE EVENTS NOR YOUR OWN MIND.

Come to think of it, if you ask me, by all accounts,
as a matter of fact, what with one thing and another,
at the end of the day, I'd have to say ...

CAN YOU REPEAT THE QUESTION?

YOUR SECRETS ARE SAFE WITH ME.

Because by tomorrow morning I won't be able to remember any of the people I've told.

I ASKED MY DATE TO MEET ME AT THE GYM TODAY. I FORGOT TO SHOW UP. THAT'S WHEN SHE KNEW WE WEREN'T GOING TO WORK OUT.

I WORRY ABOUT HAVING A <u>SENIOR MOMENT</u> IN AN ART GALLERY, MUSEUM OR TRADE FAIR BECAUSE I DON'T WANT TO MAKE AN <u>EXHIBITION OF MYSELF</u>.

DON'T YOU HATE IT WHEN PEOPLE DON'T FINISH THEIR ...

SOMETIMES, BEING A SENIOR IS JUST TRUDGING AROUND WONDERING WHAT YOU'RE FORGETTING TODAY.

• A SENIOR MOMENT IS WHEN •

FINDING THREE MILK BOTTLES IN A FIELD AND THINKING IT'S A COW'S NEST.

If I had a pound every time I had a **senior moment**, I'd be a millionaire,

AND I WOULDN'T KNOW WHY.

A Book On How To **<u>IMPROVE</u>** Your Memory Has Been Delivered, But **<u>I Don't Remember</u>** Ordering It.

ROSES ARE RED,
VIOLETS ARE BLUE.
I'VE FORGOTTEN YOUR NAME ...
AND MINE TOO.

NOTHING RUINS A FRIDAY MORNING MORE THAN REMEMBERING THAT IT'S MONDAY.

DON'T LET YOUR ENEMIES KNOW THAT YOU HAVE A BAD MEMORY; THEY'LL NEVER LET YOU FORGET IT.

My Mind Keeps **Playing Tricks** On Me, So To Get My Own Back, I've Let Down All The Tyres On My Car And **Covered The Toilet** With Cling Film.

· A SENIOR MOMENT IS WHEN ·

YOU LET THE CAT OUT AND THEN REMEMBER THAT YOU LIVE ON THE 21ST FLOOR.

Whenever I find myself in the kitchen
and don't know why, I start opening doors.

I ALWAYS BEGIN WITH THE FRIDGE.

ALL MEMORIES VANISH WHEN WE DIE.

I'm not forgetful, I'm just having an early clear-out.

MY WIFE MOCKS MY FREQUENT **MEMORY LAPSES**, BUT I'LL ALWAYS HAVE THE LAST LAUGH, BECAUSE WHAT SHE DOESN'T REALISE IS THAT I DON'T REMEMBER **EVER MEETING HER** BEFORE IN MY LIFE.

THE NEXT TIME YOU DIAL THE WRONG NUMBER, CONGRATULATE YOURSELF FOR WASTING 25 SECONDS OF A RANDOM STRANGER'S LIFE.

THE LONGER YOU LIVE, THE MORE THERE IS TO **FORGET.**

<u>Don't</u> <u>Think</u> Of Having A SENIOR MOMENT In The SUPERMARKET As Publicly Humiliating Yourself But, Rather, As <u>Gaining</u> A <u>Huge</u> <u>Tiktok</u> <u>Audience</u>.

I ALWAYS SAY TO EVERYONE,
**"WHY DON'T YOU TAKE A PHOTO;
IT'LL LAST LONGER?"**
BUT THEY JUST THINK I'M BEING SARCASTIC.

• A SENIOR MOMENT IS WHEN •

BABYSITTING YOUR FIRST GRANDCHILD – YOU REMEMBER THE CAR SEAT, STROLLER, CHANGING BAG, FEEDING BOTTLE ... AND FORGET THE BABY.

YOU TEACH ME, I FORGET. YOU SHOW ME, I FORGET. YOU BRING CAKE AND I STILL FORGET, BUT FIRST, WE PARTY!

Just because momentarily, you can't remember where you put it,

DOESN'T MEAN IT ISN'T LOST FOREVER.

MEMORIES ARE MADE OF THIS, THAT AND THE OTHER.

The trouble is, I can't remember any of that, other than this.

IF TIME IS THE THIEF OF MEMORY, THE EARS MUST BE THE SECRET GETAWAY TUNNELS.

• A SENIOR MOMENT IS WHEN •

REFUSING TO USE YOUR HEARING AIDS BECAUSE THEY ARE **VERY EXPENSIVE**, AND YOU DON'T WANT TO LOSE THEM.

Three things I most fear about growing old:
the first is losing my memory.

I CAN'T REMEMBER THE OTHER ONE.

YEARS AGO, IF SOMEONE COULD HAVE TOLD ME THAT MY MEMORY WAS GOING TO END UP LIKE MINE, I WOULDN'T HAVE <u>WASTED</u> ALL THAT TIME <u>LEARNING</u> <u>STUFF</u>.

I wonder if the person who invented the word 'senescence'
ever considered the cruel irony that it sounds like a

COOL SUPERPOWER.

• A SENIOR MOMENT IS WHEN •

YOU BREAK WIND AND BLAME THE DOG – WHO **DIED** THREE YEARS AGO.

THESE DAYS, I DON'T GET OUT MUCH; BITS OF ME FLOP OUT AND OTHERS OCCASIONALLY DROP OFF, BUT I DON'T THINK THEY COUNT.

I ALWAYS TRY TO SEE THE POSITIVE SIDE OF OLD AGE.

After all, I'm in the waiting room for heaven. Although, I do wish they'd turn up the heating.

ONE OF THE CONSEQUENCES OF BEING OLD IS THAT I DON'T COOK ANYMORE; IN FACT, EVEN DURING THE HOTTEST SUMMERS, I STILL WEAR A JACKET.

You're Never Too Old To Learn New Tricks.

Every morning I make my car keys and reading glasses disappear.

• A SENIOR MOMENT IS WHEN •
YOU STARE AT YOURSELF NAKED IN THE MIRROR UNTIL THE BUS DRIVER TELLS YOU TO SIT DOWN.

I always intended to grow old gracefully,

BUT I LEFT IT TOO LATE.

IT'S NOT THAT I DISLIKE THE YOUNGER GENERATION
BUT WHY ARE THEY ALL SO TALL?

IT'S NOT FAIR!

OLD AGE IS SOMETHING THAT CREEPS UP ON YOU WHILST YOU'RE BUSY ATTENDING THE FUNERALS OF YOUR ENEMIES.

To Keep My Old Brain Supple, I READ VORACIOUSLY – Everything Except Road Signs, Cigarette Health Warnings And The Obituaries Of All My Friends.

A healthy diet, regular exercise, great hydration, adequate sleep and above all, respecting the planet, are just **some of the things** that make the **younger generation** so

UNBEARABLE.

IN MY ADVANCING YEARS,

the single consolation of my repeated failure to diet, is that soon I'll be old and fat enough to win the EuroMillions Jackpot.

DESPITE INDULGING IN A DISSOLUTE AND PROFLIGATE LIFE, I STILL HAVE ONE WISH: THAT WHEN I DIE, BOTH MY LIFESTYLE AND MY LONGEVITY SHOULD CONFOUND ALL THE EXPERTS.

NO MATTER HOW LITTLE I THINK I KNOW, EVERY DAY THERE'S ALWAYS SOMETHING NEW TO FORGET.

THEY SAY YOU SHOULD DO ONE THING EVERY DAY THAT SCARES YOU.

So, this morning, I drove to the supermarket and back on the wrong side of the road.

• A SENIOR MOMENT IS WHEN •

YOU WALK UP TO SOMEONE IN A SINGLES BAR AND ASK, 'DO I COME HERE OFTEN?'

DON'T WASTE YOUR TIME IN ANGER, REGRETS AND GRUDGES. EXACT YOUR BRUTAL REVENGE TODAY, WHILE THE MEMORY IS FRESH.

If you can read this, Congratulations,
you can stop searching for your glasses:

YOU'RE ALREADY WEARING THEM.

YOU CAN'T REALLY KNOW WHAT'S GOING ON IN ANYBODY'S LIFE; AN **UNRELIABLE** MEMORY SIMPLY ADDS ONE MORE PERSON TO THAT LIST.

When Things Don't Go Your Way,

Remember that every challenge, every adversity
and every trivial medical complication, is something
you can tell your friends and relatives.

I'M **PREPARED TO ACCEPT** AS A BLESSING THAT I CAN ONLY EVER BE AS OLD AS I AM BUT THAT'S **NO CONSOLATION** FOR NEVER AGAIN BEING AS YOUNG AS I WAS.

INSTEAD OF MELLOWING IN OLD AGE, I'VE BECOME LESS TOLERANT; I HAVE BEEN KNOWN TO REWRITE MY WILL THREE TIMES BEFORE BREAKFAST.

I DISCOVERED RECENTLY THAT WHEN PEOPLE GET IN MY WAY, IT TAKES FEWER MUSCLES TO SMILE THAN TO HIT THE BRAKES ON A MOBILITY SCOOTER.

IF YOU LIVE LONG ENOUGH, EVENTUALLY YOU KNOW WHERE ALL THE **BODIES ARE BURIED** – LITERALLY – SO DON'T MESS WITH ME.

TO BE HONEST, I'M A BIT DISAPPOINTED WITH MY CARE HOME; I WRONGLY IMAGINED WE'D BE STAYING UP LATE DRINKING HORLICKS AND HAVING HEATED DISCUSSIONS ABOUT *ANTIQUES ROAD TRIP*.

You'd love to be able to drive, but when you turn 80 your motor insurance trebles. Also,

YOU WON'T REMEMBER WHERE YOU PARKED THE CAR.

• A SENIOR MOMENT IS WHEN •

AFTER <u>FIFTY YEARS</u> OF MARRIAGE, WAKING UP NEXT TO YOUR SPOUSE AND THINKING YOU HAD A <u>ONE-NIGHT STAND</u>.

First published in 2023 by Allsorted Ltd WD19 4BG U.K.

Author: Michael Powell
Cover design: Milestone Creative
Contents design: seagulls.net

ISBN: 9781915902115

Printed in China

10 9 8 7 6 5 4 3 2 1